This book is dedicated to all who find Nature not an adversary to conquer and destroy, but a storehouse of infinite knowledge and experience linking man to all things past and present. They know conserving the natural environment is essential to our future well-being.

BIG BEND
THE STORY BEHIND THE SCENERY®

by Carol E. Sperling

Carol E. Sperling graduated from Southern Illinois University-Edwardsville with a degree in anthropology, and has continued studies in botany and history. As a National Park Service Interpretive Ranger, Carol has worked in parks from Alaska to Big Bend, Texas.

Big Bend National Park, *located on the Texas/Mexico border on the great bend of the Rio Grande, was established in 1944 to preserve the great canyons, mountains, and desert.*

Front cover: The Sierra Del Carmen range in Mexico, beyond the Rio Grande River. Photo by Ian Shives / Aurora. Inside Front cover: The Rio Grande and the Chisos Mountains. Photo by Russ Finley. Title Page: Golden Rainbow Cactus. Photo by Robert & Linda Mitchell. Page 2/3: The Punta de la Sierra at Loop Camp along the River Road. Photo by Laurence Parent.

Edited by Mary L. Van Camp. Book design by K.C. DenDooven

Third Printing, 2009 • New Version

BIG BEND: THE STORY BEHIND THE SCENERY © 1995 KC PUBLICATIONS, INC.
"The Story Behind the Scenery"; the Eagle / Flag icon on Front Cover are registered in the U.S. Patent and Trademark Office.
LC 95-77940. ISBN 978-0-88714-101-0.

*K*nown in Mexico as La Gran Curva, or La Gran
Comba del Rio Bravo, Texans have long known what

*other Americans are just discovering—Big Bend country is
like nowhere else, and to visit once is to begin a tradition.*

The Big Bend Story

Seen from the air, the Chisos Mountains rear out of the desert plains like a craggy fortress. The coolest and moistest part of Big Bend National Park, the mountains harbor plants and animals not found in the low desert. The vast stretches of dryer lands that separate the mountain residents from others of their kind sometimes lead to speciation—the development of separate, endemic species.

Lightly visited and remote, Big Bend National Park is one of the least-known but perhaps most appreciated of the national parks. More than 100 miles from the nearest freeway, hospital, or shopping mall, travelers who make the long southward trek often stay for several days, and many return.

Visitors come to hike, to raft the Rio Grande, and to seek unusual species of birds, but for some Big Bend's greatest asset is simply its distance from anywhere else.

Encompassing a huge sweep of the northern Chihuahuan Desert, at first glance the land seems lonely and inhospitable. Soils are barren, shade is scarce, and most of an hour may pass between meeting one car on the highway and sighting the next.

It's surprising then to learn that American Indians hunted here 10,000 years ago, and that families of our grandparents' generation came to love the Big Bend as home.

Equally surprising is the tremendous variety in plant and animal life. What is this place, so close to Mexico, so far from everyday experience?

TRACY LYNCH

Havard agaves are one of about 1,200 plant species found in the park.

TOM ALGIRE

Inconspicuous until they bloom, rainbow cactus burst into flower in late spring. Unlike annual wildflowers which flower in the relative coolness of early spring, cacti tend to flower later. Perennial plants with well-established root systems, they can withstand the heat of May and June, Big Bend's hottest months.

Perhaps the most striking geologic feature in the park is the range of mountains we know as the Chisos. Rising abruptly out of the sedimentary plains, it's easy to under stand that these jagged peaks are volcanic in origin.

History in the Rocks

Ernst Tinaja continues to grow deeper and larger as occasional floods scour through the canyon. Formed in limestone, the water in the pool gradually reacts with organic material to form a very weak acid, which slowly eats away at the rock.

SCOTT T. SMITH

The geologic history written in the rocks of Big Bend National Park reveals an ever-changing and eventful past. While the oldest time periods of the Earth are not represented in the rocks of the park, there is abundant evidence of the eras when life rose and thrived—the Paleozoic, Mesozoic, and Cenozoic.

Most of the rock exposed at Big Bend is sedimentary in nature. Sedimentary rocks are those deposited as dust, sand, mud, or animal skeletons that have subsequently hardened. Limestone, sandstone, and shale are common sedimentary rocks in Big Bend, and many were deposited during the

Brilliant white ash flows, and volcanic boulders near Cerro Castellan add spectacle to the story of Big Bend's geologic past. Stacked layers of rock indicate relative age—older layers lie below younger ones. The beds of volcanic ash and volcanic boulders in the foreground are evidence of the relatively recent volcanic activity so obvious in the western portions of the park.

Cretaceous period, which lasted from about 145 to 65 million years ago. Much of what we call West Texas was covered by salty seas for most of that time, as a huge trough developed that stretched from the Arctic Sea to the Gulf of Mexico! The skeletons of countless marine animals accumulated along with lime mud on the ocean floors, gradually hardening into the thick layers of limestone that make up the walls of Santa Elena and Boquillas canyons.

Later in the Cretaceous Period, perhaps 74 million years ago, the seas receded and forests grew. Flowering plants proliferated and populations of dinosaurs and other large reptiles reached their peak. In other parts of Texas, dinosaur footprints are preserved in Cretaceous rock. In Big Bend, late Cretaceous layers of rock show evidence of climatic drying as the seas receded and forests grew and sheltered dinosaurs.

More recent layers of rock, exposed in Tornillo Flats, contain the fossils of ancient mammals that hunted and browsed in tropical swamps and forests in Early Tertiary time. Early forms of horses, camels, cats, and hippo-like animals lived and died in the wetlands that existed here about 50 million years ago.

Perhaps the most striking geologic feature in the park is the range of mountains we know as the Chisos. Rising abruptly out of the sedimentary plains, it's easy to understand that these jagged peaks are volcanic in origin. The volcanic activity that shaped the Chisos occurred between 38 and 20 million years ago, in the Eocene and Oligocene periods, and created the Davis Mountains, north of the park, as well. Two centers of volcanic activity were apparently responsible for the mountains we know today—one near Pine Canyon and the other in the Sierra Quemada, the southern foothills of the Chisos Mountains. Little evidence of the volcanic cones themselves remain, but concentric rings of intrusive igneous rocks and faults in Pine Canyon are signs of the forces that formed the Chisos.

Both extrusive and intrusive igneous rocks can be seen from the Basin—Casa Grande, Emory Peak, and Toll Mountain are parts of lava flows that once towered high above today's skyline. Pulliam, Ward, and Vernon Bailey mountains are the remnants of molten rock which squeezed up through fissures in older extrusive rocks, cooling and hardening before reaching the surface.

Other signs of volcanic activity are easy to spot throughout the park. The Grapevine Hills and the Rosillos Mountains were formed when molten rock rose along fractures in underlying rocks. Encountering an unbroken layer, the liquid rock began to force its way horizontally between sedimentary layers, forming a giant blister called a laccolith beneath the Earth's surface. Many of the prominent buttes and mesas are capped with an erosion-resistant layer of volcanic rock, which prevents the lower, softer sedimentary layers from eroding away as quickly as their uncapped neighbors. The thick bands of yellowish rock that can be seen at Burro Mesa Pouroff and in Cerro Castellan are beds of volcanic ash that solidified into a relatively soft rock called tuff.

LARRY ULRICH

Mule Ears Peaks are made of lava, and are an *example of the dramatic landforms seen in the western Big Bend that are tied to volcanic activity. Rocks that melted under the surface of the earth and later cooled are called igneous rocks—they tend to be hard and erosion-resistant.*

Sedimentary rocks are made up of debris that settles out of standing water or falls from the air before slowly hardening into stone. The Boquillas formation is limestone, formed under shallow seas from the accumulated skeletons of sea animals, mixed with mud rich in lime. Because sedimentary rocks are relatively soft, they can easily be deformed by pressure or heat from inside the earth.

Movements in the Earth's crust are processes that occur all over the world, and are probably occurring right now in your own hometown. But unless you live on an active fault zone, the movements are usually so slow that you are never aware of them. Layers of rock in Big Bend, however, show evidence of the terrific forces that lifted sections of rock hundreds of feet in the air, or dropped them down below the levels at which they were deposited.

About 300 million years ago, in the Paleozoic Era, pressures inside the Earth slowly pushed up a huge range of mountains, which subsequently eroded away or were buried in sediments over millions of years. Called the Ouachita Range, the roots of the ancient mountains can be seen near Persimmon Gap Visitor Center, near Marathon, Texas, and even in the Appalachian Mountains! More recent mountain building occurred about 62 million years ago, when the same forces that lifted the Rocky Mountains also pushed up the layers of rock that we call the Santiago Mountains and the Deadhorse Mountains in Texas, and the Sierra del Carmen and eastern Sierra Madre in Mexico. It would be correct to say, then, that two of the continent's major mountain chains—the Rockies and the Appalachians—meet in Big Bend! Basin and Range faulting continues in the area today, manifesting itself in landscapes like the escarpment at the mouth of Santa Elena Canyon.

THE POWER OF EROSION

The shaping of the continent, and of Big Bend, also continues today through the process of erosion. Like movements of the Earth's crust, erosion can be infinitesimally slow—the loss of tiny grains of sand as the wind blows across a sandstone cliff, or the occasional drop of a pebble from a canyon wall into the

Geologists call the central portions of the park the Sunken Block, referring to the displacement of rock layers caused by movement along faults. The fault at the western edge of the Sunken Block couldn't be clearer than at the mouth of Santa Elena Canyon.

river. But erosion can work with stunning speed as well—witness the power of a flash flood tearing down a desert wash after a thunderstorm. Rolling boulders, grinding pebbles, and muddy, abrasive water can change the face of an arroyo in minutes.

The most dramatic effects of erosion can be seen in Big Bend's river canyons. While geologists differ on how the Rio Grande carved Santa Elena, Mariscal, and Boquillas canyons, all agree it was the erosive force of the river that cut through hundreds of feet of rock. The route and history of the entire Rio Grande system is still being studied, but a commonly offered explanation for canyon carving is that the river was already flowing across the land as the surface began to rise. While the layers through which the canyons are carved rose at different times, the process remained the same—the river eroded downward at about the same rate that the land rose.

Other geologists suspect that the course of the Rio Grande through the park is relatively young. The interior basins of the Big Bend and northern Mexico gradually filled with sediments washed off

the rising land, and drained eastward. The ancestral Rio Grande may have flowed at this time east of the Sierra del Carmen. When the interior basins filled with enough debris to breach the Sierra del Carmen, the ancestral Rio Grande began to carve westward by headward erosion, through the accumulated sediments. Carving backwards, then, from the course of the river today, it would have first cut Boquillas Canyon, then Mariscal Canyon, and finally Santa Elena Canyon. The Rio Grande may have eventually reached the course of the ancestral Rio Conchos, flowing west of Big Bend today, and captured its flow into the newly cut route through the mountains.

While the theories differ, both assume the erosive power of the Rio Grande. The desert stream we see today seems an unlikely candidate for carving

Flash floods are seldom seen, but their evidence is all around us. Desert soils are rocky and unable to absorb much moisture. Desert thunderstorms sometimes drop more than an inch of water in less than 30 minutes. Unable to soak in, the rainwater collects in pools, then rushes downhill toward the Rio Grande. Powerful but short-lived, the floods leave a legacy of tumbled boulders, pockets of silty soil, tangled leaves, scattered seeds, and pools of water— elements of life in the desert.

TRACY LYNCH

Igneous intrusions, called dikes, cut through the foothills of the Chisos Mountains. Cracks in the layers of sedimentary surface rocks broke open, and molten lava was pushed into them like caulking is squeezed into crevices in our homes. Subsequent erosion of the upper, softer layers reveals the earth's natural caulking.

GEORGE WUERTHNER

Rainfall in the High Chisos winds its
way through a sinuous canyon before making
its final cascade into a hidden grotto of ferns,
cattails, and poison oak.

1,500-foot-deep canyons, but the river has not always been so small, and Big Bend has not always
been desert. There were long periods in Big Bend's
past when precipitation was far greater than it is today, and the river packed a much greater erosional
punch. We catch a tiny glimpse of that power when
the Rio Grande floods, as it can after wet summers.

The polished limestone at the mouth
of the Window affirms the erosive power
of water. The Window drains the entire
Chisos Basin—any moisture that falls in
the Basin or on the mountain walls that
enclose it ultimately exits through the
Window and falls into Oak Creek. Oak
Springs, in the creek bed below
the Window, is today's source of water
for the Chisos Basin development.

Then the river runs 10 to 15 feet higher than it does most of the rest of the year, and is chocolate brown with sand and grit held in suspension. Tree trunks rush by, boulders can be heard grinding along the riverbed, and old beaches are washed away to become new sand deposits downstream. How quickly would the land change if a raging, swollen river ran through it most of the time?

SUGGESTED READING

BARKER, DONALD S. *Down to Earth at Tuff Canyon, Big Bend National Park, Texas.* University of Texas at Austin, 2000.

MAXWELL, ROSS A. *The Big Bend of the Rio Grande: A Guide to the Rocks, Landscape, Geologic History, and Settlers of the Area of Big Bend National Park.* Austin: The University of Texas, 2008.

SPEARING, DARWIN. *Roadside Geology of Texas.* Missoula, Montana: Mountain Press Publishing Company, 1991.

TOM BEAN

*T*he Rio Grande flows through *the Big Bend, gathering its waters for their journey to the Gulf of Mexico. Heavily used both upstream and downstream in agriculture and industry, in Big Bend it provides moments of solitude and challenge.*

T*uff, seen on the Burro Mesa* *Pouroff Trail, may contain other rocks—volcanic bombs carried into the ash bed by explosions, or pebbles washed there by flood waters.*

P*robably named by cowboys herding* *livestock, the Boot is a spire of volcanic rock. The lava Boot is slow to erode, but wind, rain, and temperature changes are at work on it. The processes that shaped our earth continue today.*

N*ugent Mountain is framed* *by the balanced rocks on the Grapevine Hills Trail. The roundish shape of rocks in the Grapevine Hills is caused by spheroidal weathering—the syenite tends to crack and break in slightly curved patterns, and concave flakes fall away from the inner rock mass, leaving giant rounded boulders.*

JEFF GNASS

Dramatic sunlight creates variations of shapes and forms as it hits the
Rosillos Mountains from the Grapevine Hills

JEFF FOOTT

The Rio Grande is the second-longest river in North America, flowing 1,885 miles from Colorado to the Gulf of Mexico. Impounded many times and intensively used, its Big Bend character seems tranquil and pristine. Appearances can be deceiving.

The seemingly wild river of the Big Bend country is thoroughly tamed in the lower Rio Grande valley, where it provides vital water for irrigation, industry, and drinking.

JEFF GNASS

The solitude and silence in Santa Elena Canyon make it easy to forget the Rio Grande is an international boundary. Mexicans know it as el Rio Bravo del Norte, the wild river of the north.

JOHN HENLEY

The Rio Grande

NAN HURST

Mariscal Canyon conceals one of the most challenging rapids on the Rio Grande, the Tight Squeeze. While long stretches of the river are calm and nearly flat, rapids in all three canyons punctuate its tranquility with high excitement.

*The most influential factor in shaping
life in the Big Bend is the desert itself—
this is dry land, and water is
an essential element of life.*

An Abundance of Life

WENDY SHATTIL / BOB ROZINSKI

WENDY SHATTIL / BOB ROZINSKI

Look for golden-fronted woodpeckers
*year-round in the cottonwood groves
along the Rio Grande.*

Black-tailed jackrabbits use the flee and freeze technique to
*escape their predators. A quick burst of zigzag running, followed by a
motionless attempt to blend into the background, helps jackrabbits elude
hungry coyotes, bobcats, and golden eagles. It's not always successful—
jackrabbits are an important source of food for desert predators.*

Perched high above the Sierra Quemada on the South Rim, Havard agaves await the right combination of events to produce stalks of flowers. Often called century plants, they don't really live 100 years, although many species live for several decades. This species generally grows for 30-50 years before it produces a single, very large stalk of flowers. The flowering stalk grows astonishingly quickly, gaining as much as a foot a day. Yellow flowers open and are visited by insects and other animals in search of nectar. Endangered Mexican long-nosed bats in particular depend on the nectar produced by century plant flowers. As the flowers fade and the seeds mature, the agave dies, eventually falling to the ground and scattering the seeds for the next generation.

ED COOPER

JOHN ELK III

Ocotillo are often confused with members of the cactus family, perhaps because both are thorny and common in deserts. Ocotillo plants, however, are woody where cacti are fleshy and succulent; ocotillo produce true leaves after rains and cacti don't; and the flowers, when closely inspected, are very different in form. Ocotillo thorns and cactus spines serve the same protective purpose, however, by discouraging hungry desert animals. Cattle, not native to North American deserts, are not dissuaded by thorns or spines.

Big Bend National Park is one of the finest places on earth to celebrate the richness and adaptability of nature. More species of birds travel through Big Bend than through any other national park. Also, more species of cacti grow here than in any other national park. Of the desert parks, Big Bend is one of the richest in terms of plant life—more than 1,200 species of plants have been found within park boundaries. What accounts for this abundance of life in a place that looks so harsh?

Situated more or less in the center of the North American continent, Big Bend and the northern Chihuahuan desert is a meeting ground for plants and animals of both east and west, north and south. Vestiges of the last Ice Age still linger in Chihuahuan desert mountain ranges, and Douglas-fir and aspen trees survive at high elevations, reminders of the cooler and moister climate that prevailed 10,000 years ago. Such relatively recent climatic change contributes to the great diversity of life found here, and prompts some biologists to call the Chihuahuan desert an emerging desert.

The topographical variation of the area—the fact that 7,800-foot mountains are a stone's throw from the Rio Grande, flowing about 1,800 feet above sea level—creates an endless array of ecological niches, where life forms exist in the conditions that suit them best. The most influential factor, however, in shaping life in the Big Bend is the desert itself—this is dry land, and water is an essential element of life.

Big Bend is located in the northern part of the Chihuahuan Desert, the most easterly and southerly of the North American deserts. Primarily a desert of Mexico, it is characterized by a single rainy season which occurs in mid-summer. July through early October are the rainy months, when thunderstorms bring 50 percent of the year's average annual rainfall. All Chihuahuan desert lifeforms must find ways to survive the long, dry winter season.

Average annual rainfall in Big Bend ranges from about 7 inches in the low desert to more than 18 inches in the Chisos Mountains. Humidity is low, and the air has the capacity to evaporate more water from the environment than falls in most years. Temperatures are extreme, particularly in the lower elevations, where the thermometer will soar above 100 degrees Fahrenheit nearly every day for about five months of the year. Soils are rocky and alkaline, and the layer of fertile topsoil is very thin. Many of the obvious characteristics of desert plants result from adapting for these conditions.

SCOTT T. SMITH

Desert plants rarely have large, soft leaves. Exposed surface area is a disadvantage where the evaporation rate is high and sunlight is intense. Tiny leaves and some sort of protective layer to reduce evaporation losses are commonplace adaptations for desert plants. Whitish coloration helps, too, by reflecting the sun's rays away from the surface. Even the orientation of the leaves is important—by angling the broad side of the leaf away from the sun's direct rays, a plant can minimize its exposure to the drying summer sun.

Some desert plants have done away with water-costly leaves altogether—the cactus family carries on typical leaf functions in the stems and pads. The spines are really modified leaves that serve to protect and shade the plant. Ocotillo, not a cactus at all, produces leaves only in response to rain, and remains green and leafy as long as the soil is reasonably moist. When drought returns, the leaves fall off and the plant waits for the next good rainstorm. Ocotillo mimics the strategy of the cactus family—it can perform photosynthesis through its stems, whether it has leaves at the moment or not. Many

Snow brushes the Chisos Mountains *once or twice each winter. More rarely, it accumulates in the middle elevations, and only very occasionally does it fall at the river. Despite its southerly location, Big Bend is often touched by cold air masses blowing off the Great Plains. Freezing temperatures are not uncommon from November through mid-March.*

Big Bend bluebonnets are lovely reminders of *the last rainy season. Because winter rains are sparse in the Chihuahuan Desert, bluebonnets depend on moisture stored in the soil from the previous summer's rains.*

- 21 -

WENDY SHATTIL / BOB ROZINSKI

JEFF FOOTT

Tiny capsules of metabolic energy, hummingbirds move from flower to flower, harvesting the nectar produced inside. At about four inches in length, the male broad-tailed hummingbird is one of the six species that regularly visit Big Bend each summer.

Hardly bigger than a hummingbird, black-tailed gnatcatchers are insectivores. They hunt for spiders, flies, and other insects in mesquite thickets and brushy canyons.

desert plants are succulent—that is, able to store water in stems or leaves or pads. While this adaptation helps them survive long dry periods, it may also make them the food of choice for hungry, thirsty desert animals.

The root systems of desert plants are designed to maximize collection of water. Different kinds of root systems benefit plants growing in slightly different areas. The cactus family, for example, usually produces roots that grow in a netlike mass not far below the soil surface. Even light rains that barely penetrate the surface can be utilized. Desert trees like mesquite follow another strategy—some of their roots run amazingly deep to tap subsurface water sources, while others grow nearer the surface to harvest rainfall.

Diverse Animal Life

In Big Bend, as everywhere, plants provide the foundation that supports all animal life. Nearly 450 species of birds, 75 species of mammals, 67 species of amphibians and reptiles, 40 species of fish, and a host of insects find their niches in the diverse plant communities of Big Bend National Park.

Some desert animals use water more efficiently than most animals, while others are physically adapted to cope with water shortages. Kangaroo rats, for example, boast a specialized metabolism that breaks down food items, like grass seeds, into nutrients and water. Modified kidneys require minimal moisture to function, and wastes are excreted in a pasty mass. Kangaroo rats never have to take a drink of water—they obtain the moisture they need from the food they eat! Long ears and long legs can help, too. Jackrabbits dispel excess body heat via their long ears. Long legs lift an animal above the burning desert floor.

Animals also adapt to desert conditions behaviorally. Many of Big Bend's animal residents are most active between sunset and sunrise, browsing or hunting in the cooler nighttime hours. Estivation is the desert equivalent of hibernation—some desert animals sleep through the hottest or driest parts of the year, emerging only when conditions are favorable. Resting during the hottest part of the day to conserve both energy and moisture, and staying close to water sources are adaptations even humans employ.

Mexican gray wolves ranged the mountains of nearby Mexico and sometimes wandered through the Big Bend. Hunted almost to extinction by 1960, the last wild members of the sub-species were trapped in northern Mexico and taken to breeding ilities. A few Mexican gray wolves have been reintroduced into the wild in the mountains of eastern Arizona.

WENDY SHATTIL / BOB ROZINSKI

MARIE CELINO

Why would an insect sport such jewel-like colors? Perhaps as a warning. Some brightly colored butterflies taste awful—others are tasty, but look like the unpalatable ones. How's a hungry bird to know?

Many bird watchers have a fond spot in their hearts for Big Bend because of the opportunities they find here to see unusual birds. About 450 species reside in or migrate through Big Bend—nearly half of the total number of birds that live in or visit North America. You don't have to be an expert to appreciate the variety in size, shape, color, and habits of our feathered visitors!

While Big Bend's inventory of plant and animal life is impressive by any standards, there are species in peril of extinction. Some native animals, like Mexican gray wolves, are no longer seen in the park. Four animals are classified as "endangered" by the federal government: the black-capped vireo, the Big Bend gambusia, the peregrine falcon, and the Mexican long-nosed bat.

The most exciting and challenging story of an extirpated native animal's return to the park is that of the black bear. Commonly seen roaming the mountains and desert of the Big Bend until about 1940, black bears were eradicated from the area by residents who saw the bears as a threat to their livestock. Although the park was established in 1944, it took until 1988 for bears to migrate north from Mexico and rediscover their old haunts in the Chisos Mountains. Since then, a small population has taken up residence, giving visitors the chance to see bears, and the responsibility to help protect them.

TOM BEAN

Prickly pear cactus and lechuguilla survive on the dry canyon rims, but at the river's edge water-loving plants thrive.

Overleaf: Pine Canyon, on the east side of the Chisos Mountains, is excellent habitat for black bears. Photo by Jeff Gnass.

Winter brings a slowing of life processes for most plants. Prickly pear cactus often turn reddish after being nipped by frosty temperatures, as chlorophyll production drops and the plant enters an inactive stage. Annual grasses, already dry and yellow by late autumn, drop the last of their seeds. Perennial grasses, trees, and shrubs rest through the cold months, storing energy for the coming spring. Pine nuts, acorns, and mesquite beans become more important to browsing animals as green plants are less available.

The single annual rainy season of the Chihuahuan desert means that nearly every form of life must be able to tolerate long periods of drought. However, the river corridor and a few permanent springs scattered through the desert provide oases where plants and animals with high water requirements thrive. Riparian areas, where water is always available, harbor some of the most surprising plant species of the region.

Cottonwood trees, rooted deep into permanent springs, seem to burst out of the desert hills at Dugout Wells and Chilicotal. Three species of turtles make the Rio Grande their home, sunning on rocks and retreating into the water at the first sign of danger. Beavers build their lodges in the muddy banks of the river, where they are less vulnerable to the sudden flash floods that could tear a log dam and lodge apart in seconds.

The abundant moisture offered by the river and permanent springs also provides prime conditions for non-native species to become established. Tamarisk and giant river cane, both introduced to the New World in the last century, are changing the balance of life in riparian areas throughout the park.

Gurgling or trickling, desert water sources support remarkable diversity. Dragonflies flit in the humid air, mosquitoes hatch on pools of water where wasps light to drink, and swallows swoop down to feed on the same insects. Find water in the desert, and you've found a microcosm of life!

Summer rains begin with the crash of thunder and lightning—and often end with rainbows and the smell of creosote bush on the wind. Thunderheads begin to form almost daily in June, but may produce little rain until July. By mid-August, on average, brief rains are falling many afternoons, and the occasional downpour sets washes running and toads croaking.

NAN HURST

JOHN ELK III

Tamarisk, or salt cedar, is common in Big Bend and across the West. Native to the Old World, settlers planted tamarisk as heat-tolerant shade trees, only later learning that thirsty tamarisks can suck crucial water sources dry.

SUGGESTED READING

MEINZER, WYMAN. *Coyote*. University of Texas Tech Press, Texas Tech University Press, 1995.

POWELL, A. MICHAEL. *Shrubs and Trees of Trans-Pecos Texas*. Big Bend National Park, Texas: Big Bend Natural History Association, 1988.

SCHMIDLY, DAVID. *The Mammals of Texas*. University of Texas Tech Press, University of Texas at Austin, 2004.

SCHMIDLY, DAVID. *The Mammals of Trans-Pecos Texas*. A&M University Press, Texas A&M University Press, 1977

WAUER, ROLAND H. *A Field Guide to the Birds of Big Bend*. Texas Monthly Press, 1985.

WARNOCK, BARTON H. *Wildflowers of the Davis Mountains and the Marathon Basin, Texas*. Alpine, Texas: Sul Ross State University, 1977.

NAN HURST

Carmen Mountain white-tailed deer browse on succulent plants like lechuguilla and cactus, as well as tender branches.

JEFF FOOTT

Weighing about two ounces, kangaroo rats are nocturnal rodents that "beat the heat" of the desert sun by resting underground until dusk.

Striped skunks are largely nocturnal as well, hunting and scavenging under cover of darkness.

JEFF FOOTT

Javelinas are neither hogs nor boars, although they're often confused with both. Properly called collared peccaries, they are a part of a New World animal family more common in Central and South America than in the United States. Vegetarian, near-sighted and easily frightened, javelinas browse, travel, and rest in family groups of 2 to 20.

LAURENCE PARENT

The supreme predator of the air, peregrine falcons are rare and in danger of extinction. About one dozen pairs are known to nest in the park, where they produce from 6 to 20 hatchlings each year. Threatened by pesticides, hunting, and loss of habitat, they are the fastest birds on earth.

Perching on trees and tele-phone poles, red-tailed hawks are easily seen throughout North America. They patrol the mountains and deserts of the Big Bend, hunting for unwary rodents.

While most visitors to the desert fear rattlesnakes, it's the western coachwhip that most people see. They range in color from salmon to bright red, are active during the daylight hours, and move quickly, attracting our attention. Sometimes called Red Racers, Coachwhip snakes climb easily and often hunt in shrubs and trees.

Turkey vultures migrate into the Big Bend in early spring and scavenge for dead animals until returning south in late autumn. Featherless heads and a strong bill enable them to feed on carrion more easily. Perching with wings spread helps vultures maintain an even body temperature while drying and realigning their feathers.

Can roadrunners fly? They can, but they prefer to run from danger. If threatened, they may fly a few feet to perch on a tree branch. Roadrunners feed on earth-bound lizards, snakes, insects, and small rodents. Powerful leg muscles enable the roadrunner to give quick chase.

Docile and shy, tarantulas are usually seen in September when the males wander in search of females.

Burrowing owls are at home in treeless areas, and are adapted to life on or near the ground. They sometimes dig their burrows in prairie dog colonies, where they can be seen perching on a small hill or fence line post during the day, watching for careless prairie dogs.

JEFF FOOTT

The Texas banded gecko, like other geckos, has tiny suction cups on the pads of its toes.

ROBERT & LINDA MITCHELL

Alligator lizards are most common in the Chisos Mountains. Like all reptiles, they depend on their surroundings to regulate body temperature, seeking shade on hot days, and sunlight on cooler days.

MARGARET LITTLEJOHN

NAN HURST

Turtles sun on rocks along the Rio Grande, dropping into the water at the first sign of danger.

ED COOPER

Spines protect
this hedgehog
cactus—and most species of cacti—from
hungry or thirsty browsing animals.

MARGARET LITTLEJOHN

Button cacti are more common on the limestone hillsides close to the Rio Grande. Their interwoven white spines help reflect the sun's glare.

LAURENCE PARENT

Perfectly camouflaged, a
living rock cactus is almost
invisible until it blooms.

LARRY ULRICH

Red-orange flowers punctuate the
volcanic slopes of the Chisos Mountains,
where the claret cup cactus thrives.

Studded with hot pink flowers, the strawberry pitaya cactus is abundant in the foothills of the Chisos Mountains. Cacti are succulent plants— they store water in their spongy stems. The interior cells expand as moisture is absorbed after rains, and shrink during drought.

JEFF FOOTT

TOM ALGIRE

An important plant to American Indians, the fruits and young pads of prickly pear cactus can be eaten by humans.

JEFF FOOTT

Like most cacti, the outer surface of the cob cactus produces a waxy coating, which helps it conserve moisture.

The Spaniards who attempted to establish
forts along the river in the 1700s discovered,
to their terror, the consummate war skills
of the Plains people and the Apache.

Before There Was A Park

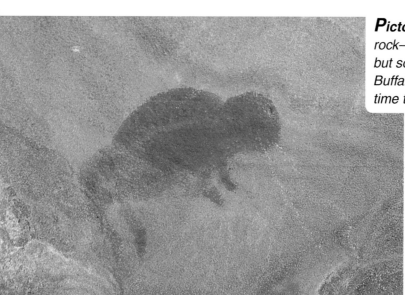

Pictographs—images painted on
rock—are impossible to interpret literally,
but sometimes speak clearly nonetheless.
Buffalo did range into the Big Bend from
time to time until the early 1800s.

TOM BEAN

TOM BEAN

Humans have used the diverse resources of the Big Bend for thousands of years. In 1993, an archaeological dig in the Chisos Basin yielded charcoal samples from a series of hearths where campfires have burned over a span of nearly 9,000 years. Those people, and later American Indians, were hunters and gatherers who moved their camps periodically throughout the year. For them, the varying elevations and diverse plant and animal communities

Mortar holes are found in many places along
the river, where American Indians ground mesquite
beans or grass seeds to feed their families. How
many hours of grinding—and how many meals—
are represented by a hole 12 inches deep?

Petroglyphs—images carved on rock—may here indicate a campsite used for generations. Ancient petroglyphs and pictographs were probably attempts to communicate, and may have marked significant sites or events. While we can find familiar symbols at other panels like this one, it's impossible to know what the carver intended.

spelled success and survival. When mountain springs shrank in the mid-winter dry season, permanent springs and lower elevations might have provided flowing water and milder temperatures.

After about 1700, Apache, Kiowa, and Comanche people came to know the Big Bend well. Hunters of the southern plains, the Kiowa and Comanche crossed the desert grasslands en route to northern Mexico. Raiding for livestock and slaves, the warriors were a constant threat to any stranger they en-

countered. The pathways by which they crossed the Big Bend and the Rio Grande were called the "Great Comanche War Trail" by later observers, who noted it was a mile wide in places, and beaten into the earth by countless hooves and feet. While the Comanche Trail is nearly invisible today, early accounts tell us it crossed the river in several places in the Big Bend country—at Lajitas, just west of Mariscal Canyon, and south of Dryden, Texas.

Part of the Great Comanche Trail crossed the Rio Grande near modern Lajitas, Texas. Situated on one of the few passable routes between Mexico and the United States in the Big Bend, Lajitas later became the site of a U.S. cavalry camp. Cavalrymen suffered from isolation, few amenities, and boredom—international incidents were rare.

The Spaniards who attempted to establish forts along the river in the 1700s discovered, to their terror, the consummate war skills of the Plains people and the Apache. Facing pressure on all sides as Europeans moved into the New World, the Apache, Comanche, and Kiowa fought tenaciously for their way of life.

Records indicate that Mexicans were establishing small landholdings, called rancherias, south of the Rio Grande as early as 1805, but few Americans had ventured into the area. In 1848, the Treaty of Guadalupe Hidalgo was signed, officially ending the Mexican-American War, and ceding California and all lands north of the Rio Grande to the United States. The new lands were vast and unknown to most Americans, and the keys to integrating them into the Union seemed to be accurate maps and a military presence.

It was the joint effort of the Boundary Commissions of both the United States and Mexico that finally succeeded in mapping the route of the Rio Grande through what we now call Big Bend National Park. The Treaty signed in 1848 called for a survey of the new border, to be completed by representatives from both governments. In 1852, Chief Surveyor William H. Emory began the survey down the Rio Grande.

Surveying the Rio Grande

On August 2, 1852, Emory ordered Tyler Wickham Chandler to take a 35-man escort, led by Lt. Duff Green, and begin surveying at Presidio del Norte, today's Presidio, Texas. His party was to head downstream along the Rio Grande until it arrived at the mouth of the Pecos River. While Chandler expected the survey to take about 100 days to cover the approximately 250 miles, it was to prove the work of two expeditions and about six months.

Chandler and Green often separated, with Chandler attempting to survey his way down the river in boats, and Green taking the men and mules over the rough terrain on one side or the other. Mules, supplies, even clothing were lost as they labored through or around Santa Elena, Mariscal, and Boquillas canyons. After more than 70 days and only 40 miles, Chandler and Green agreed near Reagan Canyon to suspend the survey.

Early in the century, Terlingua Abajo was a small but active community of Mexican floodplain farmers. They sold their grain and vegetables to the miners in Terlingua, and cut the creekside cottonwoods to fire the mine's smelters. Without the trees, soils eroded and drainage patterns changed, creating an unlikely setting for farms today.

LARRY ULRICH

The Treaty of Guadalupe Hidalgo, signed in 1848, made the Rio Grande the official boundary between Mexico and the United States. As the river's route was subsequently surveyed and mapped, politicians and businessmen hoped it would prove navigable to steamboats, reducing the costs and risks of overland wagon travel. Optimistic claims, including General Thomas J. Green's 1844 statement that "a steamboat can leave Pittsburg [sic], and go to within three hundred miles of the navigable waters of the Gulf of California," were soon disproved. Sheer canyons, rough rapids, and inaccessibility make the Rio Grande in the Big Bend the domain of recreational boaters.

The survey was completed in 1853 by another party led by Lt. Nathaniel Michler. Supported by a mule train and wagons carrying disassembled boats, Michler proceeded to the point where Chandler and Green had left the river. For some miles he avoided floating the river, but was eventually forced to unpack and assemble his boats south of today's Langtry, Texas. Warped and unwieldy, the boats careened through the rapids and smashed against rock walls, traveling in some places so quickly it was impossible to stop to make measurements for surveying. When Michler finally arrived at the mouth of the Pecos, he had, with his fellow topographical engineers, completed the survey of the parts of the Rio Grande that made up the new international boundary.

The Civil War temporarily returned the desert grasslands to the Apache and Comanche. After the war, it took nearly five years of protracted fighting with superior weapons before the military was able to move the Comanche to the Indian Territory in 1874, and not until 1881 were the Apache forced into submission.

With the completion of the Southern Pacific Railroad in 1882, cattlemen began to claim and stock land in the Big Bend. Previously unfenced and grazed only by migratory herds of native animals, the grasslands looked rich indeed. In 1885, ranch foreman James B. Gillett described Terlingua Creek as a "bold running stream, studded with cottonwood timber and...alive with beaver."

Within 20 years settlers from both sides of the Rio Grande were moving into the area. Mexican families began raising crops on the river's floodplain, and keeping a few sheep and goats. After 1910, the Mexican Revolution brought more settlers from the south, and United States cavalry troops established camps along the Rio Grande.

_H_ow must this land have appeared to early settlers? American Indians passed through the Big Bend, hunting and gathering its resources, but the Mexican and American homesteaders who arrived around the turn of the century were the first to build permanent homes and put down roots. Not everyone who settled here succeeded, and those who did struggled through prolonged drought, isolation, and the Great Depression.

JOHN ELK III

RUSS FINLEY

_G_ood health and a stunning location—what more could a man ask? For J.O. Langford, who regained his health after bathing in the Hot Springs, it was enough. A bath house and, later, motel rooms and a post office offered "the cure" to visitors until the early 1960s.

Families from the United States slowly trickled into the area, and small businesses sprang up. Tiny schools were established, often taught by local women. Several industries provided jobs and income for the growing population, as well.

Permanent occupation by cattle and goat ranchers brought big changes to the Big Bend. Ranchers actively hunted, trapped, and poisoned populations of predatory animals like mountain lions, bobcats, wolves, and bears. In rancher Homer Wilson's day, the daily wage for a ranch hand was $1, but a man could earn $25 by bringing in a lion skin. In the case of the Mexican gray wolf, extirpated from Big Bend, unable to survive in the area because of diseases borne by domestic livestock, the changes may be permanent.

While the balance of animal populations changed, so did plant populations. Pastured animals disturbed soils and grazed vegetation in ways that free-roaming native animals did not, and soil erosion and a reduction of grass cover resulted. Big Bend suffered the severe droughts of the early 1930s with the rest of the West, and ranchers, farmers, and merchants struggled through the Great Depression.

LAURENCE PARENT

Cemeteries and scattered graves mark *villages and forgotten homesteads throughout the Big Bend. Some graves are still maintained by family members who honor their dead.*

Mining began at the foot of Mariscal Mountain about 1900. Rich deposits of cinnabar—the *source of mercury—existed, and more than a few miners optimistically saw their path to sudden wealth. However, the miners, mostly poor Mexican men, discovered their work led only to exhaustion and chronic illness from mercury poisoning. Mariscal Mine produced its last flasks of mercury in 1943.*

RUSS FINLEY

Gilberto Luna and his family lived in
this simple mud and stone house. Like their
neighbors in Terlingua Abajo, they farmed
the floodplain of Terlingua Creek.

"Roosevelt's
Tree Army," the
Civilian Conservation Corps (CCC), established
camps in the Chisos Basin in the mid 30's.
Young Mexican-American, Anglo, and African-
American men enrolled from around West Texas,
and began the work of developing facilities in
what was then Big Bend State Park. They built
the Lost Mine Trail, the Chisos Basin road,
and some of the lodge buildings. Later trail
construction in the Chisos followed the CCC's
style and choice of building materials.

Before electricity, steam engines like
this one provided the power to pump water
from the Rio Grande through cotton, grain, and
vegetable fields around Castolon. From the
early 1920s until about 1941, cotton was an
important crop in
the lower Big Bend.

- 40 -

Twenty-one baths in 21 days at Hot Springs, Texas, were prescribed in the early 1900s as a virtual guarantee of returned good health. Built in 1909, the first bathhouse stood on these foundations, and was set over a hot spring that bubbled into a rock depression apparently chipped out by American Indians.

While early residents used boats to cross the river, modern Big Bend visitors use rafts and canoes to float downstream. Long stretches of tranquil water are interrupted by riffles and rapids, and occasional white water challenges even experienced boaters. From Mariscal Canyon to Langtry, Texas, the Rio Grande Wild and Scenic River runs through some of the most remote desert country in the United States.

ESTABLISHING A PARK

In 1933, the state of Texas established Texas Canyons State Park, using 15 school sections owned by the state. Lands forfeited for non-payment of taxes were quickly added and the name was changed. By October 27, 1933, Big Bend State Park included about 160,000 acres. In 1935, President Franklin D. Roosevelt signed a bill that authorized the establishment of Big Bend National Park, but acquisition of the land fell to the state of Texas. On June 6, 1944, a deed for about 700,000 acres was formally presented to President Roosevelt. Six days later, Big Bend National Park was declared officially open.

Residents had mixed feelings about the development of the national park. Some, hit hard by the Depression and the drought, sold their lands to the government with relief. Some wanted to see their lands included in the park for others to enjoy. But others, especially long-time occupants, left with sorrow and resentment, feeling forced from an area and a way of life they had come to love.

SUGGESTED READING

LANGFORD, J. O. WITH FRED GIPSON. *Big Bend: A Homesteader's Story.* Austin: The University of Texas Press, 1952.

MAXWELL, ROSS A. *Big Bend Country: A History of Big Bend National Park.* Big Bend National Park, Texas: Big Bend Natural History Association, 1985.

TYLER, RONNIE C. *The Big Bend: A History of the Last Texas Frontier.* Washington, DC: U.S. Government Printing Office, 1975.

Green Gulch is a natural passageway into the Chisos Mountains for both animals and humans. Mountain lions are more often seen here than anywhere else in the park.

All About Big Bend National Park

The Big Bend Natural History Association was founded in 1956 to help the National Park Service educate the public about the Big Bend Area. We sponsor educational and historical programs and fund scientific research projects in Big Bend National Park, the Rio Grande Wild and Scenic River, and Amistad National Recreation Area. We operate bookstores in the Visitor Centers and publish proprietary road, trail, and informational guides. Visit them at www. bigbendbookstore.org or call 432-477-2236.

Contact Us

Big Bend National Park
P.O. Box 129
Big Bend National Park, TX
79834

By Phone
(432) 477-2251

By fax
(432) 477-1175

Website
www.nps.gov/bibe

BLACK-TAILED GNATCATCHERS
PHOTO BY JEFF FOOTT

JUNIOR RANGER

Junior Rangers are special and important people. They help park rangers protect plants, animals, rocks, and historic sites. They help keep the park area clean by picking up litter and disposing of it in the proper containers.

Big Bend National Park has Junior Ranger Programs for 3 age levels. These age levels, and what needs to be accomplished in each, are found in the Junior Ranger Book that you can get from the Visitor Center.

Once you have completed the activities for your age level, return your book to the Visitor Center to be checked by a park ranger. Once the ranger signs off, you will be given your Junior Ranger badge and certificate.

TOM BEAN

River runners on the Rio Grande can expect to float for several days without sight or sound of other humans. The sounds of moving water and rustling river cane become clearer as the outside world recedes.

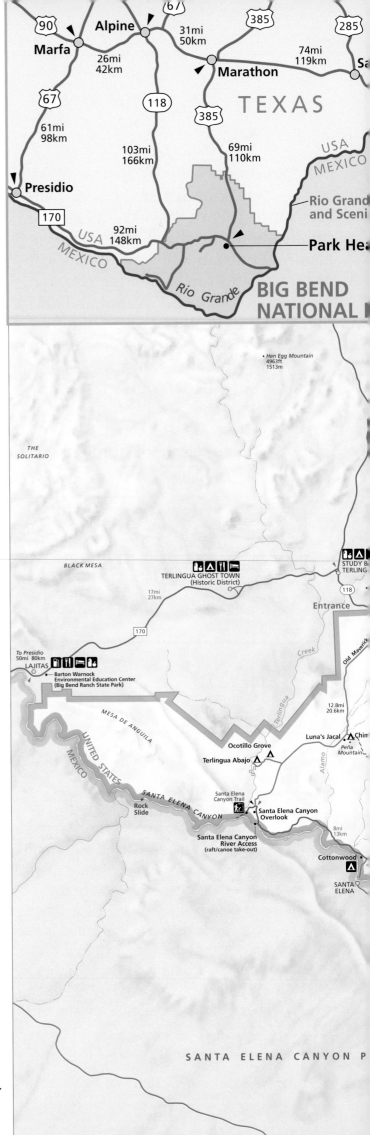

90 Alpine 67
Marfa 31mi
50km 385 285
26mi
42km Marathon 74mi
119km Sa
67 118 TEXAS
385
61mi
98km 103mi
166km 69mi
110km USA
MEXICO
Presidio Rio Grand
and Sceni
170 92mi
148km Park He
USA
MEXICO Rio Grande BIG BEND
NATIONAL

Hen Egg Mountain
4963ft
1513m

THE
SOLITARIO

BLACK MESA TERLINGUA GHOST TOWN
(Historic District) STUDY B
TERLING

17mi
27km 118

Entrance

170 Creek

To Presidio
50mi 80km
LAJITAS Old Maverick

Barton Warnock
Environmental Education Center
(Big Bend Ranch State Park) Terlingua 12.8mi
20.6km

MESA DE ANGUILA Luna's Jacal Chin

Ocotillo Grove Peña
Mountain

UNITED STATES Terlingua Abajo Alamo

MEXICO SANTA ELENA CANYON Santa Elena
Canyon Trail

Rock
Slide Santa Elena Canyon
Overlook

Santa Elena Canyon
River Access
(raft/canoe take-out) 8mi
13km

Cottonwood

SANTA
ELENA

SANTA ELENA CANYON P

- 44 -

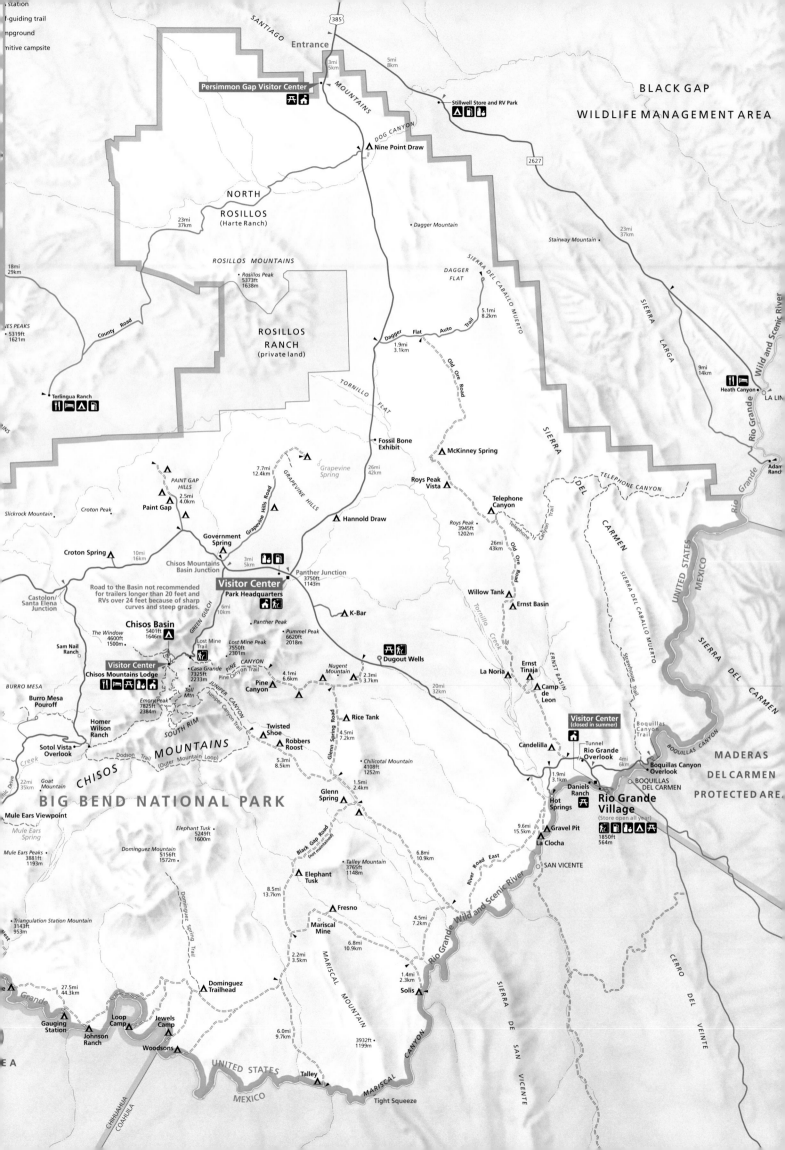

TOM ALGIRE

For 118 miles, the Rio Grande forms the boundary between Big Bend National Park and the Mexican states of Coahuila and Chihuahua. On both sides of this small desert stream, miles of lightly inhabited desert are punctuated by mountain ranges that harbor some of the region's most unusual species.

While Big Bend National Park sits firmly on the northern banks of the Rio Grande, the river does not bound the Chihuahuan Desert but bisects it. In fact, its proximity to Mexico and the resources the two countries share are part of its charm, and part of its promise. Students, researchers, rangers, and park guards from both countries— and several Latin American countries, as well—look to this national park as an opportunity to understand the complexities of life in the Chihuahuan Desert of the United States and Mexico.

Rising in Mexico just across the Rio Grande, the Sierra del Carmen are part of a new Mexican nature reserve. Big Bend National Park staff work with Mexican scientists and managers to protect the area.

Looking to the Future

Today, with fewer than 400,000 visitors each year, Big Bend continues to be lightly visited and lightly populated. For those who make the long trek south, plentiful opportunities exist for hiking, rafting, birding, photography, and enjoying the southwestern sunshine. But Big Bend is more than just a recreational park. It's also a laboratory for desert studies of all kinds, from air quality to xeric plants. Located on an international boundary, it's an opportunity for two nations to cooperate in protecting and studying one of North America's more diverse ecosystems. With nearby state preserves and Mexican reserves, Big Bend is the center of a huge area dedicated to the understanding and preservation of part of the Chihuahuan Desert.

While the land is managed by the National Park Service, the future of Big Bend really lies with every citizen. Although the park may seem insulated from the problems of urban areas, that protection is illusory. On some summer days, air quality here is the worst of that in any western national park. The Rio Grande is heavily used upstream, and pollutants flow onto silent canyon beaches. Three of the park's four endangered species are migrants—is Big Bend their last refuge on earth?

Big Bend National Park is huge and diverse. Like every natural area on an increasingly populated and technological planet, it faces pressure from development, pollution, and the thousands of visitors who find refuge from the city here. How will the next chapters of Big Bend's story develop? We and our children are the authors.

LAURENCE PARENT

Huge horizons and rugged topography are Big Bend trademarks. Lightly vegetated and vast, the framework of the earth seems easy to see.

KC Publications has been the leading publisher of colorful, interpretive books about National Park areas, public lands, Indian lands, and related subjects for over 45 years. We have 5 active series—over 125 titles—with Translation Packages in up to 8 languages for over half the areas we cover. Write, call, or visit our web site for our full-color catalog.

Our series are:

The Story Behind the Scenery® – Compelling stories of over 65 National Park areas and similar Public Land areas. Some with Translation Packages.

in pictures... Nature's Continuing Story®– A companion, pictorially oriented, series on America's National Parks. All titles have Translation Packages.

For Young Adventurers® – Dedicated to young seekers and keepers of all things wild and sacred. Explore America's Heritage from A to Z.

Voyage of Discovery® – Exploration of the expansion of the western United States.

Indian Culture and the Southwest – All about Native Americans, past and present.

To receive our full-color catalog featuring over 125 titles—Books and other related specialty products:
Call (800) 626-9673, fax (928) 684-5189, write to the address below, or visit our web sites at www.kcpublications.com

Published by KC Publications, P.O. Box 3615, Wickenburg, AZ 85358

Inside Back Cover:
The last light of day reflects off the Rio Grande.
Photo by Steve Guynes

Back Cover:
Blind Prickly Pear cactus stand as guards over the Rio Grande.
Photo by Laurence Parent

Created, Designed, and Published in the U.S.A.
Printed by Tien Wah Press (Pte.) Ltd, Singapore
Pre-Press by United Graphic Pte. Ltd